QUALITY BREWING:

A Guidebook for the Home
Production of Fine Beers

D0976545

by

BYRON BURCH

Third Edition

Joby Books
P.O. Box 2603
San Rafael, CA 94912

First Printing, October, 1974
Second Printing, December, 1974
First Printing, Second Edition, November, 1975
Second Printing, June, 1976
Third Printing, September, 1977
Fourth Printing, December, 1978
Fifth Printing, May, 1979
Sixth Printing, December, 1979
First Printing, Third Edition, July, 1980

ISBN 0-9604284-0-2

Dedication

To Alicia, Sierra, and Neva

Acknowledgments

Thanks to Peter Brehm, Art Tegger,
Leroy Wiens, Channing Rudd, Chuck
Choate, Pat McKelheer, Roxie Baird, Lee
Coe, Denis Kelly, Dayton Gould, and to
Joanne Burch, for helping, in their
various ways, to make an idea an actuality.

Photography for the third edition is by Nancy Vineyard.

INTRODUCTION

A quiet revolution has been taking place these last few years in the world of home brewing. So sweeping have been the changes that a practitioner of ten years ago would hardly recognize his craft (had he not kept up in the meantime). Fortunately the new developments have resulted in vastly better beers.

Significant advances have been made in the twin realms of technology and ingredients. The home brewer can now appropriate virtually all beneficial practices of the commercial brewery. By applying these techniques to top quality malts, hops, and yeasts, he can create superb beers. Back when "Uncle Jake" made beer in the prohibition and depression years, quantity and alcoholic strength were prime considerations, with quality coming in a poor third. This was hardly his fault, for good products and sound advice were usually unobtainable. Nevertheless, the widespread home brewing tradition fostered by Jake and his fellows has had two unfortunate, residual effects.

First, many people still believe home brewed beers must be of poor quality. This is patently false.

Second, a large body of misinformation about the brewing process is still in circulation on scraps of paper and the backs of envelopes. For example, a surprising number of people still think beer should be fermented in a warm place, though the opposite is true.

The purpose of this book, then, is to help educate, or re-educate, home brewers by providing guidance in the production of fine beers, either in one of the traditional modes, or as basic, modern, home brew. It will lead you through the mixing and boiling of the initial "wort" (your unfermented brew), and on into the "magical," living process which transforms it into finished beer.

To the beginning brewer I would suggest reading the book, trying a batch of beer using the "Procedures for Modern Home Brew" on page 3 as a guide, and then reading through the book once more. Much of the information contained herein will come into sharp focus once you've gone through the process. Many unfamiliar terms will be introduced shortly, but their meanings will become clear later on. Don't worry too much about them now.

As to supplies, most major cities in the U.S., and a number of smaller ones, now have supply shops for home brewers and winemakers. Check the Yellow Pages under "Wine Makers' Equipment & Supplies." A number of these firms are equipped to handle mail order business, which will be helpful if you live some distance away.

Note that this book gives all temperatures in Fahrenheit, with the Celsius reading in parentheses. Note also that whenever a temperature range is given for fermentation, best results will be obtained by striving for the lower end of the range. This should not discourage someone who lacks facilities for temperature control, but he should be aware that his beers can be improved by such control.

Readers in Canada and Britain will also want to note that I am using U.S. measurements. Thus a six gallon recipe is readily translated into five Imperial gallons. A table of equivalent measurements appears on page 46. Due to the onslaught of the metric system, which will soon overwhelm us all, metric equivalents are given in parentheses throughout the text whenever exact measurement is required. However, such common measurements as teaspoons, tablespoons, and cups are likely to be part of our households for quite some time, and have been retained.

American readers should note that the federal government formally legalized home brewing in 1979, and most states immediately followed suit. A single person is now permitted to make up to 100 gallons of beer each year for personal enjoyment. The head of a household is allowed 200 gallons a year. Home brewers are not required to register with the government. This is a small, but significant, advancement of human liberty, and it would seem to deserve a toast. Before an appropriate toast may be raised, however, one must learn how to make the beer.

PROCEDURES FOR MODERN HOME BREW

Dissolve *Malt Extract* and/or *Dry Malt, Citric Acid, Salt,* and *Gypsum* (if used) in one or more gallons warm *water.* Boil for 15-20 minutes. Stir in half of the *Bittering Hops,* and maintain a rolling boil for 30 minutes.* Add the rest of the *Bittering Hops,* and boil for 25 more minutes. Stir in half of the *Aromatic Hops* and boil for 5 more minutes. Place any *Corn Sugar* used (except the priming Sugar) in the primary fermentor, tie 2 layers of cheesecloth over the top of the fermentor, and place the remaining *Aromatic Hops* on it.**

Pour the boiled wort into the fermentor through the hops on the cheesecloth. Rinse the collected hops by pouring 1-2 gallons of hot *Water* through them. When the hops are cool enough, wring them out and discard. Stir the wort in the fermentor to dissolve the sugar. Stir in any *Water* still needed to bring the volume to 6 gallons. When the wort has cooled to room temperature (70°F., 21°C.), add the *Yeast* or *Yeast Starter* and *Yeast Food* (if used), and allow the wort to ferment at 60-70°F. (16-21°C.) until the Specific Gravity reaches 1.020 or slightly below. Stir the wort 1-2 times daily during the first two days of this stage.

At S.G. 1.020 siphon your brew into a secondary fermentor, attach a fermentation lock, and allow fermentation to finish. When no tiny bubbles may be seen rising in the beer when a light is held behind the jug neck, test with your saccharometer 2-3 consecutive days, if necessary, to be sure the beer is finished.

At this point you may elect to age and perhaps fine your beer (see pages 31-32), or you may go ahead and prepare it for bottling. When bottling, take your *Priming Sugar,* and make up a *Sugar Syrup* as directed on pages 33-34.

Siphon your beer back into the primary fermentor, and stir the *Sugar Syrup* in thoroughly. Stir in also the *Ascorbic Acid,* if desired (see page 27). Siphon the beer immediately into bottles, cap, and allow to carbonate for at least 3 weeks. Enjoy!

---

*Reduce the amount of hops by 25% if using hop pellets (see pages 20-21).
**If hop pellets are used as aromatic hops, you may place them directly in the primary fermentor and pour the hot wort over them. The need for cheesecloth is eliminated.

MODERN HOME BREW RECIPES

1. **Medium Bodied Light Beer — 6 U.S. gal. (22.8 liters)**

   3½ lbs. (1.6 kilos) Light Dry Malt or Light Malt Extract
   ½ tsp. Citric Acid
   1 tsp. Gypsum
   1½ tsp. Non-iodized Salt
   2 oz. (57 grams) Bittering Hops (Cluster, Talisman, or
     Cascade)
   ½ oz. (14 grams) Aromatic Hops (Cascade)
   2 lbs. (907 grams) Corn Sugar (1¼ to 1½ cups for priming)
   6 gal. (22.8 liters) Water
   1 tsp. Yeast Nutrient
   Beer Yeast or Activated Yeast Starter

   Starting S.G.   1.034-38
   Final S.G.   1.005
   Alcohol   4-4½%

2. **Medium Bodied Dark Beer — 6 U.S. gal. (22.8 liters)**

   3½ lbs. (1.6 kilos) Dark Dry Malt or Dark Malt Extract
   ½ tsp. Citric Acid
   1 tsp. Gypsum
   2 tsp. Non-iodized Salt
   2 oz. (57 grams) Bittering Hops (Cluster, Talisman, or
     Cascade)
   ½ oz. (14 grams) Aromatic Hops (Cascade)
   2½ lbs. (1.1 kilos) Corn Sugar (1¼ to 1½ cups for priming)
   6 gal. (22.8 liters) Water
   1 tsp. Yeast Nutrient
   Beer Yeast or Activated Yeast Starter

   Starting S.G.   1.036-40
   Final S.G.   1.005
   Alcohol   4½-5%

3. Medium Bodied Amber Beer – 6 U.S. gal. (22.8 liters)

3½ lbs. (1.6 kilos) Caramelized Malt Extract
½ tsp. Citric Acid
1 tsp. Gypsum
1½ tsp. Non-iodized Salt
2 oz. (57 grams) Bittering Hops (Bullion, Brewer's Gold,
  Cluster or Talisman)
½ oz. (14 grams) Aromatic Hops (Cascade)
2½ lbs. (1.1 kilos) Corn Sugar (1¼ to 1½ cups for priming)
6 gal. (22.8 liters) Water
1 tsp. Yeast Nutrient
Beer Yeast or Activated Yeast Starter

Starting S.G. 1.036
Final S.G.   1.005
Alcohol   4¼%

INTRODUCTION TO HOPPED MALT EXTRACTS

I recommend that most beginners start with the procedure and recipes on the preceding pages, as they have yielded excellent results to novices all over America. Once you've finished reading this book, you should have little trouble following the instructions. Some persons, however, will prefer working with hopped malt extracts, limiting or eliminating the use of fresh hops. If you are in this group, the following recipe and procedures should get you underway.

Recipe

3½ lbs. (1.6 kilos) Hopped Malt Extract
½ tsp. Citric Acid
1 tsp. Gypsum
1½ tsp. Non-iodized Salt
½ oz. (14 grams) Bittering Hops (Cluster or Cascade)
½ oz. (14 grams) Aromatic Hops (Cascade)
2 lbs. (907 grams) Corn Sugar (1¼ to 1½ cups for priming)
6 gal. (22.8 liters) Water
1 tsp. Yeast Nutrient
Beer Yeast or Activated Yeast Starter

Starting S.G.   1.031-33
Final S.G.   1.005
Alcohol   3½%

Procedures

This basic recipe may be used for either light or dark beer, depending on the type of malt extract used. It may also be approached in one way if you are quality oriented, and quite another if you are ease oriented.

If you desire quality, follow the Procedure for Modern Home Brew, but omit the first addition of *Flavoring Hops,* because the malt extract is already hopped. The *Flavoring Hops* called for in the above recipe are added when the second hop addition would normally be made. Everything else procedes as instructed.

If you are looking only for the easiest possible method, omit the addition of all hops from the above recipe. Draw the *Water* for your batch hot from the tap into your primary fermentor. Add your *Malt Extract, Citric Acid, Gypsum, Salt,* and *Corn Sugar* (except for the priming sugar), stirring well. When this wort has cooled to room temperature, add the *Yeast Nutrient* and *Yeast.* Follow the Procedure for Modern Home Brew the rest of the way. Be warned, however, that this method is far more likely to yield disappointing results than is the quality oriented approach.

Recipe Notes

The above recipes provide a good, basic introduction to home brewed beer. Many brewers, of course, will want to try the more full flavored, heavier bodied beers. To this end, pages 38-43 contain a number of all-malt recipes, any of which can be adapted to the basic Modern Home Brew Procedure by those not wishing to control temperatures, etc., closely enough to make the traditional beers indicated. The beers will be excellent, though a small percentage of smoothness may be lost.

Five Gallon Batches

If you prefer to make five gallons at a time rather than six, most recipes are easily adapted. If the recipe calls for corn sugar (other than that used for priming) eliminate one pound of sugar and one gallon of water. If you are working with an all malt recipe, omit about a pound of the lightest malt extract or dry malt used, and a gallon of water, and about 15% of the bittering hops.

NECESSARY EQUIPMENT

If you're a beginner reading this for the first time, you're probably bewildered by now by the mass of unfamiliar terms swarming about your head. Don't panic, though, because explanations are coming up starting here. It should also be said, for the sake of reassurance, that once you have brewed one or two batches, the basic process will be rather routine. Thus encouraged, hopefully you're ready for some detailed discussion and advice concerning equipment, ingredients, and those procedures which aren't self-explanatory. We start with the equipment.

1. A Cooking Kettle. This should be a stainless steel or enamel kettle of at least three gallon capacity, larger if possible. Other metals, such as aluminum, may give a most undesirable metallic flavor to your beer. I personally recommend stainless steel containers four gallons or larger. These are expensive but serve as a lifetime investment. Enamel tends to chip, exposing bare metal. Here, as elsewhere, the home brewer must establish his own trade-off point between ease, expense, and quality.

2. A Saccharometer. This is a hydrometer designed to measure by weight the amount of sugar in a given solution. A small amount of beer or wort is drawn off into a testing jar (graduated cylinder). The saccharometer, an elongated, hollow glass instrument weighted at the bottom and calibrated along the stem-like upper part, is placed in the liquid, spun around to dislodge air bubbles, and allowed to float freely. When it stabilizes, a reading is taken right at the surface of the liquid, at the bottom of the "meniscus," the slight clinging of the solution to the sides of the saccharometer and test jar.

Since sugar is heavier than water, though alcohol is lighter, a saccharometer, which has a constant weight, will float higher in a sugar solution (such as unfermented wort) than in plain water or an alcohol solution. The more sugar there is, the higher it floats.

The saccharometer has three functions in home brewing.

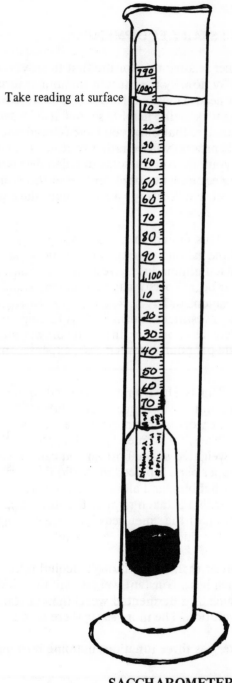

Take reading at surface

SACCHAROMETER

First, the fermentation process is yeast acting on sugar, converting it into alcohol, as well as carbon dioxide (which escapes as a gas). Therefore, measuring the amount of sugars present in the initial wort allows you to calculate in advance the potential strength of your brew. Second, floating lower and lower with each test as fermentation procedes, the saccharometer keeps track of what's happening, telling you when to siphon. Third, arriving at or near the expected final reading and stopping, it tells you when fermentation is complete much more reliably than does the mere absence of apparent activity. In short, it allows you to be much more exact about what you are doing.

Saccharometers can be calibrated according to the Balling (Brix) scale or the Specific Gravity scale. Though Balling is used in both the wine and beer industries, Specific Gravity is much more widespread among amateur winemaking and brewing books, and it is used here for that reason. Many saccharometers come calibrated with both, along with a potential alcohol scale which can be useful as well.

On the Specific Gravity scale 1.000 is the weight of water, with higher numbers indicating additional weight, such as in sugar solutions. Because the range brewers are concerned with only involves the two right hand places, it is customary to refer to these digits only to simplify communication. Thus, S.G. 1.000 is called "zero," S.G. 1.035 is "35," S.F. 1.045 is "45," and so on. This book follows the practice from here on.

If your saccharometer only gives the Balling scale, use the table on page 46 to make the conversion.

3. A Thermometer. An immersible, wide-range, dairy type thermometer with a range of roughly 20-200°F. (−7 to 94° C.) is best.

4. A Primary Fermentor. This should be an open-topped container with a capacity of at least 8-10 gallons. This will allow adequate space for the very active first stage of fermentation, including the substantial head of form that usually develops.

Primary fermentors used in home brewing are most often

either crocks or plastic wastebaskets. Crocks are aesthetically pleasing, very expensive, and quite heavy when filled. This last attribute can be significant at siphoning time. Plastic wastebaskets are modestly priced, considerably lighter in weight, and entirely adequate for home brewing use.

A word of caution is needed, though, regarding plastic containers. Don't try to save even more money by buying a real "Cheapo." When possible, buy these from a winemaking and brewing supplies dealer, as he will surely carry only "food grade" containers which won't impart a "plastic" flavor to your brew. If this is impossible, stick to name brands. Most plastic wastebaskets are now safe to use, but it's still possible to pick up an 89¢ "bargain" that will cost you beer worth ten times that amount.

Any new plastic container should be rinsed out with a small amount of bicarbonate of soda and water, and then rinsed out two or three times with clear water before its first use. This will neutralize any solvents left behind from the manufacturing process.

5. A Plastic Sheet. Tie it over the primary fermentor to guard against contamination.

6. Cheesecloth. A couple of yards are used for straining out hops.

7. A Large Stirring Spoon. Wood or stainless steel is best.

8. A Secondary Fermentor. This is one of the points at which we part company with Uncle Jake and his methods. Old style home brew was usually fermented too warm in a single, open fermentor, used baker's yeast and large amounts of cane sugar, and was consumed too young. This combination of errors produced beer with a montage of harsh, yeasty, and sour off-flavors, and gave home brew a rather unfortunate reputation in many quarters.

A prime culprit was usually oxidation, which can sour beer just as it does wine. Oxidation is caused by exposure to the air. If you've ever left a bottle of wine open for a week or so, you're familiar with what happens. Oxidation must be kept to a minimum throughout the brewing process, and the secondary fermentor is a principle weapon in the struggle. During the first, very active stage of fermentation, a great deal of carbon dioxide, escaping from the brew, protects it from contact with the air above. During the last, slower stage, however, it is advisable to provide additional protection. Therefore, at about S.G. 20, the beer is siphoned into a secondary fermentor (a jug with a narrow neck), filling or "topping up" the jug into the neck to cut down the exposed surface area. A fermentation lock is attached, and the beer is left there until fermentation is complete.

Using a "secondary" also helps out by moving the beer off of the sediment one additional time, and by making it possible to stir sugar syrup into it at bottling time without stirring up sediment. Secondary fermentors can also double as aging or lagering tanks.

I recommend the use of glass containers as secondary fermentors and aging tanks because plastic is somewhat porous, and there is some danger of oxidation right through the surface. Five gallon "water bottles" or gallon wine jugs work well.

9. Fermentation Locks. You will need one of these for each secondary fermentor. They are also called "air locks" or "bubblers," and are available through any winemaking or brewing supplier. The inexpensive, plastic, cylindrical type is quite adequate. These are partially filled with water, or preferably with sterilant ("sulphite") solution so that the bottom of the interior sleeve will be covered at all times. When fermenting in an old refrigerator with the cooling element at the top, vodka should be used instead, to keep the lock from freezing solid. A fermentation lock allows the gas pressure from fermentation to escape through the perforated cap while keeping potential contaminants away from the beer. Wine jugs with standard screwtop threads can be fitted with a screw-top holder for the lock. Other gallon jugs will normally take a bored #6 rubber stopper. Most "water bottles" will use a #6½ or #7 stopper.

10. Siphon Hose. About six feet of good hose will facilitate transfer of your brew from one container to another while disturbing the settlings and aerating the beer as little

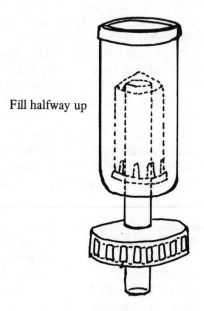

Fill halfway up

FERMENTATION LOCK

as possible. I suggest clear plastic hose with at least 3/8 inch inside diameter. Because plastic hose often tends to curl up (making it hard to reach the bottom of the container you're siphoning from) you may want to fasten it to a wooden dowel with rubber bands far enough from the bottom end that the hose is kept out of the sediment.

11. Bottles. Get good, cappable bottles of green or brown glass. Avoid no-deposit bottles as they, not being designed for re-use, tend to be made of thinner glass. If you must use clear glass bottles, make sure that your bottled beers are kept away from direct light during storage. Don't use bottles larger than you intend to pour at one time, because tipping the bottle back upright will stir up an unnecessary amount of sediment. If you like large bottles, and can't get quart beer bottles, note that most American champagne bottles are designed with a lip which will take crown caps, and these are quite serviceable.

12. A Bottle Brush. Helpful in the recycling of old bottles.

13. A Capper and Caps. Cappers come in a wide variety of styles. Get one that is durable, and that will work on the type of bottles you intend to use. Not all cappers will take all bottles. If you wish to use champagne bottles but find your capper won't take them, purchase plastic champagne stoppers and wires from your supplier and tie them down as you normally would for champagne.

OPTIONAL EQUIPMENT

In addition to the basic gear, there are some items you may want to consider because they have definite contributions to make relative to ease, precision and quality.

1. An Old Refrigerator. In some climates, and certainly for classic lagers, this item should be moved up to the preceding list, unless you are so fortunate as to have an appropriately cold cellar, ice house, or other such facility, so that fermentation and aging at the desired temperatures can be handled some other way. Some brewers cool their brews by putting their fermentors inside larger containers and surrounding them with water and ice, or by putting sealed, plastic bags of ice cubes into the primary fermentor itself. A refrigerator, however, makes chilling easier and somewhat more exact.

2. A Wine Thief or Bulb-Type Baster. This will facilitate the transfer of samples to the saccharometer test jar.

3. A Siphoning Tube. Normally this is a stiff plastic tube the end of which can be inserted into the end of your siphon hose. This extends the length of your hose and eliminates the need for a wooden dowel. Some are designed so as to gather up only a bare minimum of sediment.

4. A Hose Clamp. These are very useful when siphoning from a large container into smaller ones.

4. A Scale. Such things as hops are very difficult to measure out accurately without one of these.

6. pH Papers. These are for determining the acidity of your wort (see page 25). If possible, get narrow range papers suitable for testing from around pH 4 to pH 7.

7. Draft Beer Equipment. Should you feel eliminating the work of bottling justifies considerable cash outlay, you may wish to investigate this option. You'll need a stainless steel keg with a tap to fit it, a carbon dioxide cylinder with a pressure guage and release valve, and the appropriate fittings.

8. A Bottle Filler. The most common type is a metal tube that fits into one end of your siphon hose. At the bottom end of the tube is a spring-valve which opens when pressed onto the bottom of a bottle and closes when the pressure is withdrawn. A filler helps cut down on both messes and oxidation at bottling time.

9. A Bottle Washer. Similar in principle to the bottle filler, this device has a fitting at the upper end that allows you to affix it to a garden hose or an old style, threaded water faucet. Its use can simplify bottle rinsing.

10. Mashing and Sparging Equipment. Once you begin working with the actual malt grains as an adjunct to your wort, you will need some means of mashing and a way to rinse the grain afterward for maximum yield (see pages 30-31). Mashing may be done in your boiling kettle, in a double boiler, or in a large insulated beverage container. The rinsing or sparging may be carried out in a number of ways. Basically you need a watering can or something similar so you can sprinkle water over the grain, a pail or other container to catch it in after it passes through, and something to hold the grain while allowing the water through. One way is to use two plastic pails, stacked, with a lot of nail holes punched in the bottom of the upper one. Another way is to fit a stainless steel strainer on the top of a pail, putting the grain in the strainer. The use of a vacuum or insulated beverage jug for mashing allows for perhaps the easiest sparging method of all, as water can be added and the tap opened as many times as necessary to get a clear runoff. You'll still need a pail to catch the runoff, but this method makes the sprinkling unnecessary. In this last case, make sure you get a container designed to tolerate heat. You may wish to tie the grain loosely in a nylon mesh straining bag to facilitate its separation from the liquid.

INGREDIENTS

At least as important as the equipment you choose, of course, are the ingredients which comprise the beer itself. Vast improvements have been made in this area in recent years, which make it necessary to discuss the various ingredients and the functions they perform. For convenience, we can group them into six categories: malts, sugars, hops, yeasts, water and water treatment, and optional refinements.

1. Malts. These could be grouped with the sugars as "fermentables," for both provide sugar which yeast can convert. Malt, however, is a far more complex subject than are the other sugars, and there is considerable difference in the way it is treated. Malt exists at the very heart of brewing, for the malty flavor it gives combines with the bitterness and aromatics of the hops to form the basis of any true beer. Body, also, comes from the malt. Most sugars, on the other hand, serve primarily to raise the alcohol content of a beer while doing little, if anything, for the body and flavor. Thus, if you prefer full bodied, full flavored beers in the European style, you will want to try brews with a high malt content, severely limiting the use of other sugars, or eliminating them entirely, except at bottling time.

Though other grains can be malted, most brewers use the term "malt" only in reference to malted barley. In the malting process the grain is allowed to partially sprout. Then it is kiln-dried at lower or higher temperatures, depending on whether a lighter or a darker malt is desired. Malting begins the multi-step process by which the starches in the grain are converted into fermentable sugars. The process is completed by the "mashing" procedure, in which the grain is crushed, water is added, and the mixture is cooked at a number of particular temperatures for specified periods of time in order to convert the various starches.

Fortunately, the home brewer doesn't need to go through all of that in order to brew excellent beers. A number of reasonably priced, high quality, concentrated extracts of malt are currently on the market in either syrup or powder form.

These are concentrated from malt after it has been mashed, so the home brewer is spared that rather involved process. For ease in differentiation, I call the concentrated syrups "malt extracts," and the powdered form, "dry malt."

Up to this point, the best quality malt extracts and dry malts have been those from Britain, with a few good ones coming from Canada. For many years American brewers relied on domestic malt extracts not specifically designed for home brewing, and their lack of options was reflected in the results they obtained. With the situation in the U.S. having loosened up somewhat recently, though, I am hopeful that top quality domestic malts will soon become available. If so, by all means try them. It is also hoped that good German extracts will make their appearance, so they may be submitted to exhaustive tests.

In any case, both light and dark malt extracts and dry malts of good quality may now be obtained. Also some caramelized extracts, such as Edme S.F.X. (plain), and John Bull Bitter (hopped), are available.

Should you have access to the actual malted barley, you may want to try some beers using the grain in small amounts along with malt extract or dry malt in order to provide greater complexity of flavors. To do this, follow the simplified "Mashing for Flavor Procedure" on pages 30-31. Malt grain is usually available to home brewers as "pale malted barley," "crystal malt," and "black patent malt."

Pale Malted Barley is exactly what the name suggests. It can be used in small amounts to add body and flavor to any type of brew, or to raise slightly the Specific Gravity of a wort. It is also the primary malt used in beers made "from scratch" by advanced brewers.

Crystal (caramel) Malt is kiln-dried at a higher temperature than is pale malt, and this gives it its darker color and caramelized flavor. It is used in relatively small amounts for adding color and flavor to amber, brown, or dark beers.

It should be noted that the term, "crystal malt," is not really accurate when referring to caramelized, brown grain malt. True crystal malt is much paler. However, "crystal malt" is well embedded in the home brewing literature in reference to caramel malt, and most suppliers use the term this way in their packaging as well. For this reason I'll stick with it, though the term "caramel malt," would be more correct.

Black Patent Malt is very dark and strong flavored. It is used in dark beers and stouts. Unlike the other malt grains, it is not normally crushed or put through a mashing proce- dure, and should have no appreciable effect on the amount or "fermentables" in your wort. Black Patent is added whole to the wort during boiling. I recommend starting out with very small amounts and increasing the ratio in successive batches until the level is reached that suits your taste. Used with re- straint, it can yield good results, but it should be crushed by only the more masochistic among us.

A number of other specialty malts are used by commercial brewers, and these could become available to amateurs if enough demand develops. For example, *Munich Malt* has re- cently appeared in my area. It has a fine flavor and a pale gol- den color. It may be used in place of crystal malt or pale malted barley for a somewhat different effect.

2. Sugars. Simply expressed, the fermentation process is yeast acting on the sugars present in the wort, dividing them into roughly equal parts of alcohol and carbon dioxide. Thus, the amount of sugar present determines the final alcohol con- tent. In brews where only malt is used, all the alcohol is de- rived from malt sugar (maltose). In others, when a lighter bodied, less malty beer is desired, other sugars may be used to supplement a smaller amount of malt. In most cases, sugar will at least be used at bottling time to carbonate the brew. Four types of non-malt sugars are worthy of mention.

Corn Sugar (Dextrose) is the sugar most extensively used in quality home brewing. It is readily fermentable and carries less potential for off-flavors than cane sugar. Note, though, that either corn or cane sugar used in large amounts may give your beer a "cidery" taste. If you find this disagreeable, stick to beers with a high malt content, and little sugar.

Cane Sugar (Sucrose) will produce slightly more alcohol per pound than corn sugar, but it must be inverted by the yeast before fermentation can begin. Because a residual sour- ness can result, cane sugar is best used only if inverted first. To do this, add about two pounds (or one kilo) of granulated sugar to about a pint of water. Stir in about a quarter tea-spoon of Citric Acid, heat while stirring, and hold at about 212° F. (100°C.) for about 30 minutes. The resulting syrup may be added immediately to the wort or used after cooling. Remember to allow for the water used when figuring the total volume of the wort. Note also that Cane Sugar will give you a slightly higher gravity per pound than Corn Sugar (see page 45).

Milk Sugar (Lactose) is non-fermentable, and can therefore be used to sweeten certain stouts when this is desired.

Brown Sugar (or Molasses) can be used in small amounts for flavoring dark ales.

3. Hops. When brewers speak of hops, they refer to the flowers of the female hop plant *(humulus lupulus)*. It is these which are harvested, dried, and used in beermaking.

Hops serve as a preservative, and as a flavoring and aromatic agent. I find it useful to distinguish between "bittering hops" and "aromatic hops," though in practice this distinction is somewhat obscured.

Bittering Hops are so designated because during the preparation of the wort they are boiled along with the malt for 60-90 minutes, during which time bitter resins are extracted from the hops, which give a pleasingly bitter flavor to the beer. This is the first major step if you are working with malt extract or dry malt, and the second (after mashing and sparging) if you are using grain. In practice, some of these hops are boiled for the full time, and others are added a bit later. As the hops are boiled with the malt, the hop resins released into the wort afford a measure of protection for your brew against certain potential contaminants.

It should be mentioned here that *Hop Extracts* in liquid form are frequently available. Used as directed, they may be substituted for all or part of your bittering hops.

A superior alternative, however, is the use of *Hop Pellets,* a relatively recent development with wide commercial acceptance. The pellets, which look like rabbit food, are mechanically extracted from fresh hops, and therefore retain the fresh hop flavor and aromatics exceedingly well. With extraneous matter removed, a pound of hops is reduced down to 10-12 ounces. Thus, when substituting pellets for fresh hops, reduce the amount used by one-fourth, or slightly more. Pellets are easy to use. They are stirred into the boiling wort in the same way as are fresh hops, but they do not need to be strained out with cheesecloth at the end. They will settle out during fermentation and storage. This settling can take quite some time, however, so you may wish to fine beers made with the pellets.

Remember that hop flavored malt extracts may be used with good results (see page 6). Note that the hops in a hop flavored malt may have been added either by the above described boiling process or by mixing. To date, only one manufacturer of these malts (Edme) actually states in its literature that its hopped extracts (called "concentrated worts") are already boiled with the hops. Until more information is forthcoming, it is safest to boil the others as you normally would. As for the concentrated worts, they need not be boiled at all if a highly simplified method is what you want, but I find results are more to my liking if they are at least boiled long enough to add a small amount of fresh aromatic hops.

Aromatic Hops play an important role in the production of any good beer. They are added to the wort near the end of the boiling process so that their fresh character is maintained. Their purpose is to add the glorious flavor and aroma of fresh hops to your beer. Choose your freshest and most aromatic hops for this purpose.

In the last few years, the most revolutionary development in home brewing has been in the quality and variety of available hops. When Uncle Jake brewed, he most often had to rely entirely on hopped malt extract. If he had hops at all, they were usually highly compressed hops, packaged in a small cake or brick. They are still around and may be used as bittering hops, but unless your supplier is impervious to change, you shouldn't have to rely on them. Top grade hops have become available in a number of varieties for the amateur brewer. The availability of specific types will probably vary from time to time and from place to place, but in my area we've become familiar with a number of varieties.

Cluster is a variety widely grown in the United States. It rates medium high in bitterness and has a characteristic taste which some home brewers don't particularly care for, but it serves acceptably as a bittering hop or in blends. Early Cluster is the specific type most often available to home brewers. Late Cluster is somewhat less bitter.

Talisman is an improved cluster variety. It rates roughly the same as Early Cluster in bitterness. It is a top grade bittering hop.

Brewer's Gold is a strong, full-flavored hop, high in bitterness, suitable either as an aromatic or bittering hop in your most aggressive ales and stouts.

Bullion, a sister strain of Brewer's Gold, has very similar characteristics. They may be used interchangeably by the home brewer. This is, in fact, an extremely common practice in the brewing industry.

Fuggle has a spicy, though mild, aroma, and is quite low in bitterness. It makes a fine aromatic hop.

Cascade, low in bitterness, with an extremely pleasant aromatic character, is probably as good an aromatic hop as you're likely to find. It is a new hybrid just coming into large scale production. The reason for the enthusiastic reception it has received is that, unlike other varieties, it fully retains its continental character when grown in North America. This fact makes it the hop to use for your finest lagers at all stages.

Northern Brewer, a full, bitter, fragrant hop, is excellent in ales and steam beer.

The recipes in this book suggest particular varieties. The selections reflect personal taste, and are in no way intended as definitive statements. Should you have other varieties where you are, try them out. The recipes are only intended as suggestions to get you started. With hops and malts particularly, you will no doubt want to start experimenting as soon as you have acquired a measure of experience and a degree of self-confidence. The recipes are good ones, but they've never been inscribed on stone tablets and hand carried down from Mt. Sinai, at least so far as I know. Remember that one advantage of home brewing is the potential for arriving at your own personal beer, answerable only to your individual taste. As far as hops are concerned, just remember that more bittering hops will give you more bitterness, while more aromatic hops will increase the fresh hop flavor and aroma, and that some varieties are more bitter or more flavorful and aromatic than others (see pages 44-45).

4. Yeast. This, of course, is the living organism that makes the whole brewing process work. The yeast you use, therefore, should be selected with some care. The basic rule here is to use only a good quality, active beer yeast. Baker's yeast should only be used if there is absolutely no alternative. The fact that many old recipes call for it is inevitable, as it is only recently that beer yeast has become widely available. It is also true that beer yeast and baker's yeast descend from the same ancestral strain, *S. Cerevisiae,* and that both baker's yeast and top-fermenting beer yeast are still officially designated by this same term, but this is misleading. By means of mutation and selection over millions of yeast generations, the two industries have evolved yeasts vastly different in character. Beer yeast, for example, can be used in making bread, but it would probably take up to five or six times as long for the bread to raise. By the same token, baker's yeast, used in brewing, tends to ferment at an erratic pace, and often lends a strong, yeasty flavor to the beer. It settles out poorly, and that which does settle is easily disturbed when the beer is poured. Beer yeast can be purchased inexpensively enough that no one should still be sabotaging their product with an inferior yeast.

One more cautionary note is necessary. Brewers' yeast, as sold in bulk by health food stores, has been deactivated (killed) and will not work. Any fermentation you happen to get will stem from "wild" yeasts of undetermined character.

There are two basic kinds of true beer yeast, the top-fermenting ale type, and the bottom-fermenting lager type.

Top-Fermenting Yeast has, of course, been traditionally used for British type beers. Less expensive and hardier than bottom yeast, it makes an excellent all-purpose brewing yeast for ordinary home brew, as well as your more distinguished ales and stouts. As the term, "top-fermenting," indicates, fermentation takes place at or near the surface.

Bottom-Fermenting Yeast was originally a variant sub-strain of *Cerevisiae,* but it has now earned its own name,

"S. Carlsbergensis." This is the true lager yeast of the Conti-
nent. The most delicate of all wine and beer yeasts, it is nonetheless admirably suited for cold (40-55° F. or 5-13° C.) fermentations. It is used for all lagers, as well as for San Francisco steam beer. When buying a lager yeast, make sure you get
what you pay for. Look for the words "lager," "bottom-fermenting," or *"S. Carlsbergensis."* "Beer yeast," especially if
it comes from Britain, is most unlikely to be a lager yeast.

Beer yeasts are packaged either in dry form or as liquid
cultures. I tend to prefer the dry, which seems to have a better "shelf life" (A pox on yeast companies who don't date
their packages). Whatever form and type of yeast you use, it
is a good idea to make up a yeast starter a couple of days in
advance of "pitching the wort" (adding the yeast). This is
particularly true with delicate lager yeasts. Making a starter
builds up the culture in advance so that a strong fermentation
can begin as soon as possible after the wort is prepared. The
reason this is important is that until fermentation begins,
your wort has no protection against oxidation caused by surface exposure to the air. Escaping carbon dioxide takes care
of the problem, so it's best to get fermentation underway
quickly. Directions for making a starter are on page 31.

If you are using an ale yeast, you may just add the yeast
directly to the wort, omitting the starter, as these tend to begin fermenting more rapidly. In this case, dissolve the yeast in
a cup of warm to lukewarm water for about 10 minutes before pitching the wort.

In any case, pitch as soon as the wort has cooled to about
70° F. (21° C.) and cool the wort to the desired temperature
as soon as active fermentation begins.

5. Water and Water Treatment. There are many types of water
supplies, and these will be variously suitable for brewing. As a
general rule, brewing water should be relatively hard, but more
or less neutral in taste. If your water supply is strongly flavored, you may want to use bottled spring water, either partially or entirely, for your brewing. If you have water which
is quite soft, or are using distilled water, you will probably
wish to harden it.

Most home brewers use small amounts of *Gypsum* to

harden water. One or two teaspoons, added at the time the wort is boiled, are generally adequate for the purpose, though your own taste, once again, is the final arbiter. Pale ales are normally brewed with somewhat harder water than are other beers, and may require more gypsum.

Non-iodized Salt serves in brewing as a flavor enhancer. If you do much cooking, you are no doubt familiar with this attribute of salt, and know how small amounts of it are used in such unlikely places as cakes and egg nogs to the same end. Use about 1½ teaspoons for 5-6 gallons of light beer, and up to twice that amount for very dark beers. Non-iodized salt is specified as even small amounts of iodine could inhibit fermentation.

Citric Acid (commercial brewers may use phosphoric, or even sulfuric) is also added to the wort at boiling time, primarily to raise the level of acidity (lower the pH). One-half teaspoon will normally suffice for 5-6 gallons. If you wish more precision, purchase some pH test papers and make your own adjustments. A pH of 5 to 5.2 is ideal for mashing or for your unfermented wort. If you start in this range, your final pH, after fermentation, will be below 4.5, which is considered a safe level in food processing. Because dangerous bacteria, such as botulism, can't survive in an acid medium, proper acidity can build an insurance policy into your beer. Citric acid is widely available, and normally has a pleasant taste. Should you detect a slight lemon flavor or acid aftertaste in your beer, cut back slightly on the amount. It probably stems from a relatively low pH in your water supply.

6. Optional Refinements. This, as you might expect, is rather a catch-all, covering some things which don't fit neatly into the other categories, but which are helpful nonetheless.

Yeast Nutrient, Food, Energizer, or *Brewing Salt* can be used to make your wort a more conducive medium for active fermentation. As the variety of names suggests, a number of such products are available from various suppliers, and the precise formulations are as individual as the names. In general, however, the basic ingredient will be either ammonium phosphate or ammonium sulphate, with such things as Vitamin B-1, Koji, Epsom Salt, and/or Urea possibly included as well.

Such products are listed as optional because malt alone provides an excellent yeast medium. Thus, a wort using at least 5 lbs. (2.3 kilos) of malt extract or 4 lbs. (1.8 kilos) of dry malt in a 5-6 gallon batch will very rarely need additional boosting. With a lower malt content, a teaspoon or so of one of these products, added with the yeast or yeast starter, can help speed up the onset of fermentation, and prevent "stuck fermentations," in which the yeast stops working with the job only partially done.

Koji, or *Aspergillus Oryzae,* is an enzyme that converts grain starch to fermentable sugar. It is traditionally used in the conversion of rice for/sake, but can be very useful with barley malts as well. It may be added either after mashing, or after boiling the wort, as soon as the mash or wort has cooled to at least 135-6° F. (58° C.). Take a cup or two of water, and stir in about half a tablespoon of koji for each pound (1 Tbl. per kilo) of malt grain used. Heat the mixture to 135-6° F. and stir into the mash or wort. If adding it to your mash, hold the temperature of the entire mash at 135-6°F. for about 10 minutes before proceding to sparge.

The complex of enzymes contained in malt grains themselves, and which effects the conversion of starches into fermentable sugars, is commonly called *Diastase* or *Amylase.* You may purchase this separately as well, and add it directly to the mash. Half a teaspoon per pound of grain should suffice.

The use of either koji or diastase as directed, and a mash of 45 minutes or so, should eliminate the need for an iodine starch test when mashing only a pound or so of malt grain for purposes of color and flavor.

Unmalted Barley is sometimes pre-cracked, flaked, and sold as "Flaked Barley." You may wish to use it for an extra crispness of flavor. Normally, one pound is sufficient for 5-6 gallons of beer, and smaller amounts are often used to good effect. Follow the "Mashing for Flavor Procedure" on pages 30-31, except that five parts of diastatic malt syrup (such as Edme D.M.S.) should be included in the mash for every part of unmalted barley.

An alternative method is to use koji or diastase as instructed above, and reduce the amount of diastatic malt syrup
by one-half. In any case, sparge as usual. Note that the flaked
barley is rather difficult to sparge efficiently.

Ascorbic Acid (Vitamin C) is often added to beer either
before aging or at bottling time as an anti-oxidant. Half a teaspoon to 5-6 gallons is sufficient. Its purpose is to protect the
beer against the air trapped in the bottle or aging tank. This
is a particularly good idea if all or some of the beer will re-
main in storage for some time before being consumed. Note
that only pure ascorbic acid should be used. Vitamin C tablets contain only minute quantities of the pure stuff, sup-
plemented with a lot of unknown buffers that can leave you
with an insoluble, cloudy haze in your beer. This may be to
your taste, but it's not to mine.

Ascorbic acid has been increasing in price lately, and supply has been somewhat uncertain at times. Consequently,
some suppliers are looking to other anti-oxidants. *Sodium
Erythorbate* is already on the market in my area. It is used
in the same manner and proportions as ascorbic acid.

Fining Gelatin and Grape Tannin may be used in combination for a process called "fining," which can give your beer
more clarity than the unaided settling process can provide.
Fining (see page 32) is done during aging, after the secondary
fermentation is complete. Only the clear, unflavored type of
gelatin should be used.

A Heading Agent may be used to give your brew a somewhat longer lasting head when poured than is otherwise possible. A number of such preparations have been in use by commercial breweries, especially since detergents have become
widely used for cleaning glassware. Whatever heading agent
your supplier stocks, use as directed.

Irish Moss, actually a powdered seaweed preparation, can
significantly improve the settling qualities of the beer. Stir one
teaspoon into the wort about halfway through the boiling
process.

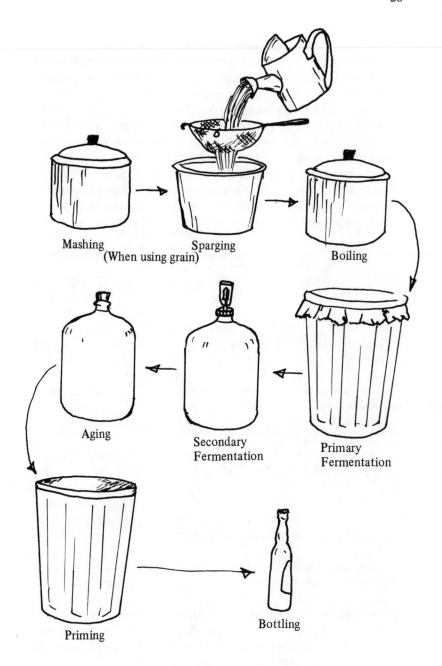

Mashing
(When using grain)

Sparging

Boiling

Primary
Fermentation

Secondary
Fermentation

Aging

Priming

Bottling

HOME BREWING PROCEDURES

PROCEDURES

If you chose to explore the earlier cross-references before continuing with your reading about equipment and ingredients, you will already be somewhat familiar with this section. You will also have begun to see that the "whats," the "whys," and the "hows" of home brewing are hopelessly interrelated. There is a process, of course, to match up with every ingredient and every piece of equipment. Some processes are self-explanatory. Others have already been clarified in the preceding two sections. A third group, however, requires more extensive comment, and to this group we now turn.

1. Sterilization. This is one of the most important aspects of good brewing practice. Unfortunately, when most people think of sterilization or general cleanliness, boiling water, soaps, and detergents spring to mind. None of these methods, however, should be applied to your brewing equipment. Boiling melts plastic, cracks crocks, and weakens glass bottles. Soaps and detergents leave invisible residues, virtually impossible to rinse away, which can flavor your beer most unpleasantly, and interfere with its ability to form and hold a head.

Chlorine is the most widely used sterilant for home brewing equipment. Some suppliers pack chlorine detergents for this purpose. If you use one of these products, follow the directions, of course.

An alternative is to mix 1½ tablespoons of household, chlorine bleach thoroughly into a gallon of cold water. Use a small amount of this mixture to rinse out all of your equipment before each use. Follow with 2-3 thorough rinses with clear water to avoid inhibiting your yeast and giving your beer a chlorine taste. Beer bottles are sterilized in the same manner.

You may store chlorine solution for up to a month by keeping it tightly stoppered, in a cool, dark place.

Sodium Bisulphite, so widely used in winemaking, is also an excellent alternative to chlorine as a sterilant for your brewing equipment. Well stoppered, a "sulphite" solution retains its effectiveness 4-6 months, and it requires only one or

A simple method of sparging small amounts of mashed grain, collecting the water in the boiling pot.

Adding the malt extract.

Gypsum and other water treatment items are added.

Hops are needed to round out the brew. In this case, hop pellets are being used.

The wort is boiled, stirring occasionally, and more hops are added at appropriate intervals.

The wort has just been poured into the primary fermentor where it will be covered and allowed to cool.

When the wort has cooled, a specific gravity reading is taken.

You're then ready to add the yeast starter.

The plastic cover sheet has been removed to reveal an active primary fermentation with foam and resinous material rising to the surface.

When the specific gravity is around 1.020, the beer is siphoned into the secondary fermentor.

Secondary fermentation continues until no tiny bubbles can be seen rising into the neck of the jug. A specific gravity reading is taken to confirm that the beer is ready to bottle.

The beer has been siphoned back into the primary fermentor and priming sugar has been stirred in. It's now ready to be siphoned into bottles, capped, and set aside to carbonate.

This is really what it's all about. The optimum time for savoring your beer, by the way, is while you're cooking up a new batch.

two rinses with clear water after use, being less likely than chlorine to adversely flavor your beer in trace amounts.

A stock solution is easily made up by dissolving an ounce (28 grams) of sodium bisulphite crystals in a quart (.95 liters) of water. Equipment and bottles are rinsed with the solution and then with water. In winemaking, sulphite is added directly to the batch to sterilize the ingredients as well, but this is not done in brewing, as sulphite can create problems of its own in amounts large enough to effectively sterilize the wort. There are, however, two situations in which sulphite may be added directly in smaller amounts, but for different reasons.

First, if your water supply is excessively chlorinated, you may neutralize the chlorine by drawing your brewing water into open containers a day or so before use, and stirring in one tablespoon of stock sulphite solution per gallon. Cover loosely until ready to use. Boiling, however, will accomplish the same thing, and will sterilize as well.

Second, if ascorbic acid is unavailable, you may use sodium bisulphite as an anti-oxidant in its place. For 6 gallons of beer, stir in 1 tablespoon of your stock sodium bisulphite solution as the boiling of the wort begins.

Sodium bisulphite crystals can be found at any winemaking and brewing supply shop.

2. Mashing for Flavor. As mentioned earlier, the mashing process when making beers from scratch is quite involved. When using small amounts of grain malts, primarily for additional flavor to supplement malt extract or dry malt, however, a simplified version of the procedure can be used.

Crack your grain, using a rolling pin, coffee grinder, or slow-speed blender. Loosely tie the cracked grain in cheesecloth, and cover it with water. It is best, at this point, to stir in a small amount of your citric acid and gypsum. The percentage used should correspond roughly to the percentage of your brewing water being used to cover the grain. In other words, if you are making 6 gallons of beer, and using a gallon of water for your mash, one-sixth of the citric acid and gypsum called for in the recipe should be added here.

Heat the mash to 150° F. (65° C.) and hold at that temperature as exactly as possible for 45 minutes to an hour. The permissible range is 145-155° F. (63-68° C.). Don't go higher or you may kill off the starch converting enzymes. You may assist the mashing process by adding 1-2 lbs. of diastatic malt extract to the mash as you begin, or by using koji or diastase as directed on page 26.

After mashing, you may wish to test for unconverted starch. Put a few drops of the water from the mash into a white or clear glass, and add a couple of drops of iodine diluted with water. A color change to blue generally indicates the presence of unconverted starch, and the mashing procedure should be continued for an additional hour if necessary. Be sure and discard all test samples.

After mashing, the grain must be rinsed off, or *sparged.* Pour off the free liquid, and spread out the grain across the bottom of your perforated pail, strainer, or beverage jug (see page 16). Slowly sprinkle 160° F. (71° C.) water over the grain until the water which passes into the lower container is clear. Add this to the water previously poured off, and use this liquid in the boiling of the wort. Discard the spent grain.

3. Preparing a Yeast Starter. Two days before you intend to start a new batch, or bottle a beer that is lagering, dissolve about 4 tablespoons of malt extract or dry malt in a quart of water, and boil for five minutes. When the mixture has cooled to about 70° F. (21° C.), place it in a sterile gallon or half-gallon jug, add a package of yeast, and seal the jug with a fermentation lock. Store at room temperature for at least one full day before pitching the wort.

4. Skimming. During primary fermentation, a head of foam normally develops. Some brewers like to skim away the dark, gummy resins that gather at the foam's surface. I don't feel this is necessary, except perhaps, for your most delicately flavored light beers.

5. Lagering or Aging. Good beers, like good wines, will improve with further aging after fermentation has ceased, though the changes, in this case, take place more rapidly, and are subtle enough that many home brewers will skip this process in their anxiety to consume their wares. Nonetheless, aging is beneficial to most beers, and essential for true lagers. Beer should be aged in closed, tightly stoppered containers which are filled up into the necks.

Lagers get their name from the long, cold aging (lagering) process these beers undergo. They are aged, or lagered, at 32-33° F. (0° C.) for a period of 3-6 months. If your beers must be aged at a temperature warmer than 40° F. (4° C.), you would best be advised to leave them in aging containers only long enough to allow your finings to settle out. Further aging could take place in the bottle where the presence of carbon dioxide virtually eliminates the risk of any unwanted infection.

6. Fining. While aging or lagering your beer, you may very well wish to fine it to achieve maximum brilliance and clarity. I personally feel finings should be added at the start of the aging process because this requires the least handling of the beer. They can be used, however, at any time as long as at least 10 days are allowed for them to settle out.

Stir a teaspoon of unflavored gelatin into 10-12 oz. (about one large water glass) of water, and let it set for a half hour. Siphon your beer into an open container. Heat the gelatin and water to 180° F. (83° C.) and stir until the gelatin is dissolved. Stir it directly into the beer, and siphon the beer into a closed container for aging. Gelatin will combine with tannin, provided by the hops, and settle out impurities. Stirring in ¼ teaspoon of grape tannin before adding the gelatin can be beneficial to the process.

7. Saving Yeast. There is no need to buy yeast for each new batch unless you lack appropriate storage facilities. The best place from which to take yeast for your next batch is from the bottom of your secondary fermentor. Most of the resinous substances and the yeast cells which are either dead or very weak will have been left behind in the primary fermentor, so that a relatively pure, healthy yeast culture can be found in the secondary. The optimum situation, of course, is to have a new wort ready to be pitched just as you remove your beer from the secondary. Simply stir up the yeast and add it to the new batch.

If your new wort is not ready, fill a sterile, pressure resistant bottle up to half full with yeast, top up with finished, flat beer, and store under refrigeration, as close to 32-33° F. (0-1° C.) as possible. Yeast may be kept, tightly stoppered, for over a week this way. Loosen the stopper immediately upon removing it from the refrigerator.

Keep in mind always that yeast goes through many generations in a short time, and it is possible for mutations to occur which may have adverse effects. Should you begin having less than ideal results with no readily apparent cause, try changing your yeast culture, especially if it has been used three or more times. Remember also that contamination or excessively long storage could cause souring. Always check a stored culture for any signs of this by smelling it before use.

8. Carbonation. Home brewed beers are carbonated by the time-honored method of allowing a limited amount of fermentation to take place in sealed bottles. This time the fermentation's objective is to produce, and trap, the carbon dioxide, though there is also a slight increase in alcohol.

Uncle Jake's approach was to quickly bottle the still fermenting beer when the gravity dropped to the appropriate level. Unfortunately, this is a bit tricky, unless you are quite experienced, and the desired point can be reached as easily at 3 a.m. as at any other time. Therefore, such varied results as flat beer, all night bottling sessions, or blown bottles and sticky messes, were relatively common. Any of these can be discouraging to brewers, and the last most certainly discourages their wives. Happily, such problems are easily avoided.

The simplest, and most common, modern method of carbonating home brewed beers is to allow the beer to ferment completely out. Once the beer is flat, you can add a measured amount of sugar to prime it for just the right amount of carbonation. A ratio of ¼ cup of corn sugar per gallon, or a small amount less, best suits American taste. The best way to add it is to stir 1½ cups corn sugar into 1-2 cups of water. Heat it to boiling, stirring occasionally, boil for five minutes, and let it cool. Boiling turns the mixture into a syrup. Siphon your beer into an open container, and stir the sugar syrup in well. You may add ascorbic acid at this point also, if this has not already been done. Siphon the beer immediately into bottles and cap them.

Should you taste a beer you are about to prime, and feel it needs additional hop flavor and aroma, you may make a correction by an alternative priming method. Measure out two cups of water and stir in ¼-½ oz. fresh hops. Heat to boiling and boil for five minutes. Strain out the hops through cheesecloth, wringing them out when they are cool enough. Stir the corn sugar into this hopped water, heat once again to boiling, and proceed as in the preceding method.

After you've gained some experience, you may wish to try the traditional priming method known as kraeusening, assuming the name hasn't scared you off. It simply means priming a finished beer by adding to it a small amount of a new wort which has just begun fermenting. Add enough wort to raise the gravity of the beer you are bottling by six points (eight points if you are using an all-malt wort). For example, if your saccharometer shows that your beer has fermented all the way down to zero (1.000), it should be raised to either six (1.006), or to eight (1.008), depending on the type of wort used. The reason for the difference will be made clear in the discussion of final gravities which follows shortly.

Whichever priming method you use, your bottled beers should be stored for at least three weeks to allow full carbonation to take place. Note also that if the beer you are priming has been aged or lagered for some time after fermentation, and particularly if it has been fined, it may be necessary to add a new yeast starter along with your sugar syrup for priming, in order to insure an adequate culture of healthy yeast to carbonate the brew. If you are kraeusening, of course, the yeast present in the fermenting wort will be sufficient, and a starter will not be necesssary.

If your beer has been lagering, you would also be well advised to allow it to warm to roughly the same temperature as the area in which it will subsequently be stored before putting it into bottles. This will keep heat expansion from adding unduly to the natural carbonation pressure that develops in the bottle.

9. Final Gravities. If you have skipped ahead and looked at the all-malt recipes on the pages coming up, you may have noticed that the final gravities listed are quite a bit higher than those for recipes using both malt and sugar in the wort. Worts with a malt/sugar ratio ranging between one to one and two to three, will normally gravity down to approximately zero (1.000). As this ratio is increased (more malt and/or less sugar is used), the final gravity you may expect also goes up in relatively direct proportion until, with an all-malt wort, it reaches a point which is roughly one-fourth the starting gravity of the wort. Thus, you may calculate the expected final gravity of most all-malt worts by dividing the starting gravity by four.

All this may seem frighteningly complex, but it really isn't if you remember that the saccharometer doesn't measure sugar directly, but infers it by indicating the weight of a solution. In introducing the saccharometer, it was mentioned that sugar is heavier than water, but alcohol is lighter. It stands to reason then, that if you ferment a solution of pure, highly refined sugar, the gravity will start out above 1.000 and finish below it, down toward .990. Malt, however, is not so highly refined, and contains additional elements which provide body (and weight). Thus, more malt means more weight and a higher final gravity, but more alcohol derived from a refined sugar lowers the final gravity.

This should explain why beers with a high sugar content may finish up somewhere around the zero point, though high-malt beers terminate somewhat higher. By derivation, you should also be able to see why it is necessary to raise the gravity an extra two points to obtain the desired amount of carbonation when kraeusening with an all-malt wort.

Note that a very black beer may finish up a bit higher. The reason is that a black malt, such as black patent, has all or most of the fermentables burned out of it when it is kilned. It can still add other elements to a wort, increasing the percentage of non-fermentables, and thereby raising the final gravity. In most cases, dividing the starting gravity of the wort by three should set the upper limit of the final gravity range for these beers, though stouts may gravity out a bit higher. It is obvious that you should look for visible signs of fermentation, and also taste the beer to see if any untoward sweetness remains. If you have serious doubts about whether a given batch is finished, get a urine sugar analysis kit (the kind used by diabetics) from the drug store, and use it to test for residual sugar. Some brewing supply shops may carry these kits as well. One percent sugar is roughly equal to four gravity points. If your beer has stopped fermenting and contains more than .5% sugar, add a new yeast or yeast starter when you prime it in case your fermentation is stuck, and decrease your priming sugar to compensate.

10. Serving. All home brewed beers have a bit of sediment at the bottom of the bottle. Some may regard this as a minor annoyance, but I find it part of the beer's charm, a constant reminder of its natural origin. In any case, sediment is not particularly pleasant to taste. Therefore, your beer should be poured slowly into a tilted glass until the sediment begins to rise into the neck of the bottle. You then tip the bottle upright again so as not to allow the sediment to pass. As a skilled hand will waste very few drops of beer in the process, rigorous practice is suggested.

Sit back then, and enjoy the fruit of your labors. Such a moment combines the enjoyment of good beer, the fulfillment of your creative urge, and the achievement of a bit more independence than is often possible in modern life.

PROCEDURE FOR ALES AND STOUTS

This is essentially the same as the basic "Procedure for Modern Home Brew" on page. 3.*

Always use a top fermenting yeast for these beers. Ideal fermentation temperature is 55-60° F. (13-16° C.).

Ale and Stout Recipes

1. Medium Bodied Pale Ale — 6 U.S. gal. (22.8 liters)

3½ lbs. (1.6 kilos) Light Dry Malt or Malt Extract
½ lb. (227 grams) Crystal Malt
½ tsp. Citric Acid
1-2 tsp. Gypsum
½ tsp. Non-iodized Salt
2 oz. (57 grams) Bittering Hops (Brewer's Gold, Bullion, or Northern Brewer)
½ oz. (14 grams) Aromatic Hops (Fuggle or Cascade)
6 gal. (22.8 liters) Water
2 lbs. (907 grams) Corn Sugar (1¼ to 1½ cups for priming)
1 tsp. Yeast Nutrient
Ale Yeast

Starting S.G.	35-40
Final S.G.	5-6
Alcohol	4-4½%

---

*If pale malted barley or crystal malt are used, follow the "Mashing for Flavor" procedure on pages 30-31, prior to boiling the wort. Use the resulting liquor in the boiling. If black patent malt is used, add it uncrushed, about halfway through the boiling of the wort, and strain it out when boiling is completed.

2. Full Bodied Pale Ale — 6 U.S. gal. (22.8 liters)

6 lbs. (2.7 kilos) Light Dry Malt or 7 lbs. (3.2 kilos) Light
   Malt Extract
½ lb. (227 grams) Crystal Malt
1-2 tsp. Gypsum
½ tsp. Non-iodized Salt
2 oz. (57 grams) Bittering Hops (Brewer's Gold, Bullion, or
   Northern Brewer)
½ oz. (14 grams) Aromatic Hops (Fuggle or Cascade)
6 gal. (22.8 liters) Water
1¼ to 1½ cups Corn Sugar (for priming)
Ale Yeast

Starting S.G.   44-46
Final S.G.   11-12
Alcohol   4%

3. Full Bodied Brown Bitter Ale — 6 U.S. gal. (22.8 liters)

6½ lbs. (3 kilos) Caramelized Malt Extract*
1 lb. (454 grams) Crystal Malt
1 tsp. Gypsum
2 tsp. Non-iodized Salt
½ lb. (227 grams) Brown Sugar (optional)
2 oz. (57 grams) Bittering Hops (Brewer's Gold, Bullion, or
   Northern Brewer)
2½ oz. (71 grams) Aromatic Hops (Fuggle, Cascade, or
   Talisman)
6 gal. (22.8 liters) Water
1¼ to 1½ cups Corn Sugar (for priming)
Ale Yeast

Starting S.G.   42
Final S.G.   10
Alcohol   4%

---

*This can be an excellent recipe to introduce you to the idea of using
hopped malt extracts in full bodied beers. If using hopped extract, such
as John Bull Bitter, reduce the amount of flavoring hops to 1 oz. (28
grams), and follow the instructions on page 6.

4. Simple Stout − 6 U.S. gal. (22.8 liters)

7 lbs. (3.2 kilos) Concentrated Stout Wort (hopped)
1½ tsp. Non-iodized Salt
1½ oz. (43 grams) Aromatic Hops (Fuggle or Cascade)
6 gal. (22.8 liters) Water
1¼ to 1½ cups Corn Sugar (for priming)
Ale Yeast

Starting S.G.   42-43
Final S.G.   10-11
Alcohol   4%

5. Irish Type Stout − 6 U.S. gal. (22.8 liters)

5 lbs. (2.3 kilos) Light Dry Malt or 6 lbs. (2.7 kilos) Light
    Malt Extract
2 lbs. (907 grams) Caramelized or Dark Malt Extract
1 lb. (454 grams) Black Patent Malt
2 tsp. Non-iodized Salt
2½ oz. (71 grams) Bittering Hops (Brewer's Gold, Bullion, or
    Northern Brewer)
½ oz. (14 grams) Aromatic Hops (Fuggle or Cascade)
6 gal. (22.8 liters) Water
1¼ to 1½ cups Corn Sugar (for priming)
Ale Yeast

Starting S.G.   48-50
Final S.G.   12-20
Alcohol   4½-5%

PROCEDURE FOR LAGERS

This is essentially the same as the basic "Procedure for Modern Home Brew" on page 3, with the following changes.*

Pitch with a bottom-fermenting yeast starter, When active fermentation begins, cool the wort, and ferment at 40-50° F. (5-10° C.).

When fermentation is complete, siphon into an open container and add ascorbic acid and finings, if desired. Siphon immediately into a closed container, and lager (age) for 3-6 months at 32-33° F. (0-1° C.). When bottling, prime by kraeusening if you wish.

Lager Recipes

1. Full Bodied Dark Lager — 6 U.S. gal. (22.8 liters)
4 lbs. (1.8 kilos) Light or Caramelized Malt Extract
3 lbs. (1.4 kilos) Dark Dry Malt
1 tsp. Gypsum
2 tsp. Non-iodized Salt
1½ oz. (43 grams) Bittering Hops (Cluster, Talisman, or Cascade)
1½ oz. (43 grams) Aromatic Hops (Cascade)
6 gal. (22.8 liters) Water
1¼ to 1½ cups Corn Sugar (for priming) unless you are kraeusening
Lager Yeast Starter

Starting S.G.   47
Final S.G.   11-12
Alcohol   4½%

---

*If pale malted barley or crystal malt are used, follow the "Mashing for Flavor" procedure on pages 30-31, prior to boiling the wort. Use the resulting liquor in the boiling. If black patent malt is used, add it uncrushed, about halfway through the boiling of the wort, and strain it out when boiling is completed.

2. Full Bodied Light Lager — 6 U.S. gal. (22.8 liters)

2 lbs. (907 grams) Light Malt Extract

5 lbs. (2.3 kilos) Light Dry Malt or 6 additional lbs. (2.7 kilos) Light Malt Extract

1 lb. (454 grams) Pale Malted Barley

1 tsp. Gypsum

1½ tsp. Non-iodized Salt

1½ oz. (43 grams) Bittering Hops (Cluster, Talisman, or Cascade)

½ oz. (14 grams) Aromatic Hops (Cascade)

6 gal. (22.8 liters) Water

1¼ to 1½ cups Corn Sugar (for priming) unless you are kraeusening

Lager Yeast Starter

Starting S.G.   49-52
Final S.G.   12-14
Alcohol   5%

3. Full Bodied Amber Lager — 6 U.S. gal. (22.8 liters)

2 lbs. (907 grams) Light Malt Extract

5 lbs. (2.3 kilos) Light Dry Malt or 6 additional lbs. (2.7 kilos) Light Malt Extract

1 lb. (454 grams) Crystal Malt

1 tsp. Gypsum

1½ tsp. Non-iodized Salt

1½ oz. (43 grams) Bittering Hops (Cluster, Talisman, or Cascade)

1½ oz. (43 grams) Aromatic Hops (Cascade)

6 gal. (22.8 liters) Water

1¼ to 1½ cups Corn Sugar (for priming) unless you are kraeusening

Lager Yeast Starter

Starting S.G.   50-52
Final S.G.   12-14
Alcohol   5%

BACKGROUND AND PROCEDURES FOR STEAM BEER

If you've ever been to San Francisco, you may have encountered Anchor Steam Beer, the only remaining representative of a California brewing tradition which dates back to the time of the Gold Rush, and the only all-malt beer produced in the United States. If so, you will probably be most anxious to brew steam beer yourself, especially if you live outside the Bay Area, where Anchor is distributed.

Steam beer is a peculiarly American brew, born as an alternative to lager, back when no transcontinental railroad existed, and ice for cooling lagering cellars would have had to come "around the Horn." Steam beer is fermented at cellar temperature (about 60° F. or 15° C.) rather than at room temperature (70° F. or 21° C.) as is commonly thought. A bottom-fermenting yeast starter is used. Steam beer is traditionally a draft beer, primed in the keg by kraeusening. The resulting pressure in the keg came to be called "steam," and this led to the term, "steam beer." To really be authentic, then, you will need draft beer equipment, but you may modify this and kraeusen at bottling time instead. Other procedures are carried out in the usual manner.

Steam Beer Recipes

1. Simple Steam Beer – 6 U.S. gal. (22.8 liters)
  7 lbs. (3.2 kilos) Caramelized Malt Extract
  1½ tsp. Non-iodized Salt
  2½ oz. (71 grams) Bittering Hops (Cluster, Talisman,
    Brewer's Gold, Bullion, or Northern Brewer)
  ½ oz. (14 grams) Aromatic Hops (Cascade)
  6 gal. (22.8 liters) Water
  Lager Yeast Starter

  Starting S.G.   39
  Final S.G.   10-11
  Alcohol   4%

43

2. Steam Beer – 6 U.S. gal. (22.8 liters)

5 lbs. (2.3 kilos) Light Dry Malt or 6 lbs. (2.7 kilos)
Light Malt Extract
1 lb. (454 grams) Crystal Malt
1½ tsp. Non-iodized Salt
2½ oz. (71 grams) Bittering Hops (Cluster, Talisman,
Brewer's Gold, Bullion, or Northern Brewer)
½ oz. (14 grams) Aromatic Hops (Cascade)
6 gal. (22.8 liters) Water
Lager Yeast Starter

Starting S.G.	39
Final S.G.	9-10
Alcohol	3¾%

PROHIBITION STYLE HOME BREW

Perhaps someday you'll be in a rather bizarre mood, and get curious about what home brewing used to be like. That would be the time to try this recipe. It, and others very much like it, are still in circulation. I've seen a number of them.

3 lbs. (1.4 kilos) any Blue Ribbon Hopped Malt Extract
10 lbs. (4.5 kilos) Cane Sugar
10 gals. (37.9 liters) Water
Baker's Yeast

Dissolve the Malt Extract and Sugar in warm water. When it gets down to about room temperature, add the Yeast (place the yeast on a piece of rye bread, if you must, and float it on the surface of the wort). Ferment at room temperature in an open fermentor. Siphon into bottles and cap them when the beer gravities down to 5. Store for at least 5 days.

FORMULATING YOUR OWN RECIPES

This is not particularly difficult, and you'll undoubtedly want to give it a try. As a general guideline, I would suggest a minimum of 2½ lbs. of malt extract, and a maximum of 3½ lbs. of corn sugar for a 6 gallon batch. Hops, of course, may be increased or decreased according to taste. You may also change varieties, or blend a number of types, to achieve particular effects. The following tables may assist your calculations.

Advanced Hop Data

Hops can be as complex a subject as you wish to make it. To be really precise, you would have to know, not only the hop variety, but the particular vintage, and where they were grown as well, just as with wine grapes. The amount of lupulic (alpha) and lupulinic (beta) acids present determines the degree of bitterness in a given batch of hops, and the amount of essential oils determines the degree of aromatics. The particular variety you are using determines the type of flavor and aroma you will get. I can't tell you about specific hop vintages you're likely to encounter in the future, but here are the most recent figures available for the more common hop varieties grown in the U.S., showing the average alpha and beta acid contents of the individual varieties, as well as the average amounts of essential oils. You may find the table useful when changing varieties for a given recipe, or when blending several types for increased complexity. The acid figures represent percentages of acids found in a given sample of good quality dried hops. Note that beta acids contribute only 10% as much bitterness as a like amount of alpha acids. The oil figures represent milliliters per 100 grams of dried hops.

Variety	Alpha	Beta	Oil
Early Cluster	7.5-8.0	5.5-6.0	1.0
Late Cluster	5.5-7.5	4.5-6.0	1.0
Fuggle	4.0-6.0	2.5-4.0	1.0
Bullion	8.5-11.0	4.5-5.5	2.5
Brewer's Gold	8.5-11.0	4.5-5.5	2.5
Talisman	7.5-9.0	4.0-5.0	1.0
Cascade	5.0-6.5	5.0-6.5	1.5
Hallertauer	5.0-6.5	4.0-6.0	1.0
Tettnanger	5.0-6.5	4.5-6.5	1.0
Comet	9.5-10.5	3.5-4.5	1.5
Northern Brewer	9.5-10.5	4.0-5.0	1.5

Malt and Sugar Values

   With one pound of the following ingredients per gallon of water, you may reasonably expect the following gravities:

Ingredient	Gravity
Corn Sugar	36
Cane Sugar	45
Brown Sugar	45
Edme Malt Extracts	36*
John Bull Malt Extracts	36*
Gold Medal Malt Extracts	36*
DCL Malt Extracts	34*
Blue Ribbon Malt Extracts	34*
Dry Malt	45*
Pale Malted Barley	24†
Crystal (caramel) Malt	15†
Munich Malt	20†

*Somewhat variable
†Quite variable

Specific Gravity and Balling Equivalents

Balling	S.G.	Balling	S.G.
0	1.000	11	1.044
1	1.004	12	1.048
2	1.008	13	1.053
3	1.012	14	1.057
4	1.016	15	1.061
5	1.020	16	1.065
6	1.024	17	1.070
7	1.028	18	1.074
8	1.032	19	1.078
9	1.036	20	1.083
10	1.040		

Weight and Measure Equivalents

Fluid Measure

1 imperial gallon = 1.2 U.S. gallons (4.5459 liters)
1 U.S. gallon = .833 imperial gallon (3.7853 liters)
1 imperial fl. oz. = .961 U.S. fl. oz.
1 U.S. fl. oz. = 1.041 imperial fl. oz.
1 imperial pint = 20 imperial fl. oz.
1 U.S. pint = 16 U.S. fl. oz.
1 U.S. cup = 8 U.S. fl. oz. (.5 U.S. pint, .417 imperial pint)

Weight Measure

There is no difference between U.S. and imperial weights.

1 oz. = 28.35 grams
1 lb. (16 oz.) - 453.592 grams (.45359 kilograms)
1 kilogram (1,000 grams) = 35.274 oz. (2.2046 lbs.)

Converting Fahrenheit to Celsius

To convert a Fahrenheit temperature reading to Celsius, subtract 32 from the Fahrenheit figure, and divide the result by 1.8.

Saccharometer Temperature Correction

Most saccharometers you will encounter are set to read correctly at 60° F. (16° C.). If your beer is not at that temperature, you should correct accordingly by adding or subtracting specific gravity points as indicated in the following table.

Temperature in degrees F.	Correction Needed
50	Subtract ½
60	Read as shown
70	Add 1
77	Add 2
84	Add 3
95	Add 5
105	Add 7

It is the philosophy of this book to provide the basic information needed for successful brewing, and to give you some recipes to introduce the various types of beers. Now you should start experimenting. You may well come up with a variation you like even better than the original version. Here's an example to demonstrate how far this experimentation may be taken. Versions of this recipe have dominated the stout classifications in two of the three judgings in which they have been entered, including the first international home brew competition in April of 1980. It was developed by two friends of mine, Dr. John Bolton of Mill Valley, California, who made the first batch, and his advisor, Steve Norris, owner of The Home Brew Company in San Francisco.

Be advised that this recipe should not be attempted by someone who's not sure he has the taste for very dark, bitter stouts.

Dr. John's Stout — 12½ U.S. gal. (47.3 liters)

18 lbs. (8.2 kilos) Hopped Dark Malt Extract
2¼ lbs. (1 kilo) Plain Light Malt Extract
2 lbs. (907 grams) Crystal Malt
1 lb. (454 grams) Black Patent Malt (cracked)
Bittering Hops: 4 oz. (113 grams) Cluster Hop Pellets *and*
   3 oz. (85 grams) Bullion or Brewer's Gold Hop Pellets
Aromatic Hops: 4½ oz. (128 grams) Cascade Hop Pellets
2 tsp. Non-iodized Salt
12½ gal. (47.3 liters) Water (preferably soft)
Ale Yeast

This beer should start at about S.G. 55, and finish at about 15-20. However, John didn't stop there. After preparing the wort, he separated out about 2½ gallons to which he added two pounds of Corn Sugar, bringing the S.G. up to 90. This batch was fermented down to about S.G. 15 using Champagne strain wine yeast because this yeast tolerates high alcohol concentrations. The resulting brew is rather like a concealed weapon. Try it if you must, but a Surgeon General's warning on the bottle would probably be in order.

ADVANCED MASHING TECHNIQUES

If and when you get to the point of working entirely or
in large part, with grain malts, you will need some additional
sophistication in the area of mashing. British books on home
brewing can be somewhat misleading in this area, because
their malt grains are more completely converted, or modified,
than are ours in North America. Unfortunately, our malts require treatment that is somewhat more extensive.

When working with British malts, you simply mix together
your cracked malt grains, water to cover them (up to 60% of
your brewing water, with the remainder in reserve for sparging),
and Citric Acid and Gypsum in proportion to the water used.
This mash is gradually heated to 150° F. (65-66° C.), and held
at that temperature for up to two hours. Sparge in the usual
way. This is the traditional British "infusion" system of mashing, but it should be used with American malts only when no
more than a pound or so of grain is used with 5-6 gallons of
beer for color and flavor.

With American grain malts, you must go through some
additional steps not necessary with their British counterparts.
The mash is first raised to 95-100° F. (35-38° C.), and held
there for 30 minutes. It is then raised to 113° F. (45° C.), and
held for an hour. Raise it again to 135° F. (57.5° C.), and hold
for 20-30 minutes. Raise it then to 150° F. (65-66° C.) and
hold for 45 minutes to an hour. Finally, raise it to 170° F.
(77° C.) for 10 minutes prior to sparging. This is our version
of the "infusion" mashing system. Infusion is traditional for
ales, stouts, and steam beers.

The traditional mashing method for lagers is called "decoc-
tion." In this method, the various temperatures are achieved
by removing a percentage of the water from the mash, heating
it to boiling, and returning it to the mash to raise the temperature of the whole. Whichever method you wish to employ,
diastase or koji may be used to help the process along.

Working straight from the grain is not for everyone, but
should you wish to try it, you will be one step closer to na-
ture, and to the ghosts of those prehistoric people who started
mankind on the road to fine beer.

SUGGESTED FURTHER READING

Anderson, Stanley, with Hull, Raymond. *The Art of Making Beer.* New York: Hawthorn Books, Inc., 1971.

Berry, C.J.J. *Home Brewed Beers and Stouts.* 6th ed. Andover, England: The Amateur Winemaker, 1971.

Coe, Lee. *The Beginner's Home Brew Book.* Portland, Oregon: S.B. Taylor and Associates, 1972.

Eckhardt, Fred. *A Treatise on Lager Beers.* rev. ed. Portland, Oregon: Hobby Winemaker, 1972.

Eckhardt, Fred. *A Treatise on Lager Beers. An Outline of Advanced Beermaking Procedures.* privately printed, 1972.

Hopkins, R.H., and Krause, C.B. *Biochemistry Applied to Malting and Brewing.* London: George Allen and Unwin Ltd., 1937.

Hough, J.S., Briggs, D.E., and Stevens, R. *Malting and Brewing Science.* London: Chapman and Hall Ltd., 1971.

Line, Dave. *The Big Book of Brewing.* Andover, England: The Amateur Winemaker, 1974.

Shales, Ken. *Advanced Home Brewing.* Andover, England: The Amateur Winemaker, 1972.

INDEX

Index (cont'd.)

Mr. Burch is well known on the West Coast for his expertise
in the area of home made beers and wines. He managed
Wine and the People for three years and has exchanged ideas
with hundreds of home brewers. He has given lectures on
beer and wine in a number of cities. He is a co-owner of
Great Fermentations, a supply shop for home brewers with
outlets in San Rafael and Santa Rosa, California.